Union Public Library
W9-BBV-059

HIP-HOP

Hip-Hop

Pharrell Williams

Terrell Brown

Union Public Library

Mason Crest Publishers

Pharrell Williams

FRONTIS Writer, producer, performer, and fashion icon, Pharrell Williams is a
multitalented star. And to think, his solo career is just beginning!

PRODUCED BY 21ST CENTURY PUBLISHING AND COMMUNICATIONS, INC.

EDITORIAL BY HARDING HOUSE PUBLISHING SERVICES, INC.

Copyright © 2007 by Mason Crest Publishers. All rights reserved. No part of this
publication may be reproduced or transmitted in any form or by any means,
electronic or mechanical, including photocopying, recording, taping, or any
information storage and retrieval system, without permission from the publisher.

MASON CREST PUBLISHERS INC.
370 Reed Road
Broomall, Pennsylvania 19008
(866)MCP-BOOK (toll free)
www.masoncrest.com

Printed in Malaysia.

9 8 7 6 5 4 3 2

Library of Congress Cataloging-in-Publication Data

Brown, Terrell.
   Pharrell Williams / by Terrell Brown.
      p. cm. — (Hip-hop)
   Includes bibliographical references (p.   ) and index.
ISBN 1-4222-0125-2
   1. Williams, Pharrell—Juvenile literature. 2. Rap musicians—United States—
Biography—Juvenile literature. I. Title. II. Series.
ML3930.W55B76 2007
782.421649092—dc22
[B]   2006013612

Publisher's notes:
- All quotations in this book come from original sources, and contain the spelling
  and grammatical inconsistencies of the original text.

- The Web sites mentioned in this book were active at the time of publication.
  The publisher is not responsible for Web sites that have changed their addresses
  or discontinued operation since the date of publication. The publisher will review
  and update the Web site addresses each time the book is reprinted.

Contents

Hip-Hop Timeline

1974 Hip-hop pioneer Afrika Bambaataa organizes the Universal Zulu Nation.

1988 *Yo! MTV Raps* premieres on MTV.

1970s Hip-hop as a cultural movement begins in the Bronx, New York City.

1985 *Krush Groove*, a hip-hop film about Def Jam Recordings, is released featuring Run-D.M.C., Kurtis Blow, LL Cool J, and the Beastie Boys.

1970s DJ Kool Herc pioneers the use of breaks, isolations, and repeats using two turntables.

1979 The Sugarhill Gang's song "Rapper's Delight" is the first hip-hop single to go gold.

1986 Run-D.M.C. are the first rappers to appear on the cover of *Rolling Stone* magazine.

1970   **1980**   **1988**

1976 Grandmaster Flash & the Furious Five pioneer hip-hop MCing and freestyle battles.

1986 Beastie Boys' album *Licensed to Ill* is released and becomes the best-selling rap album of the 1980s.

1970s Break dancing emerges at parties and in public places in New York City.

1982 Afrika Bambaataa embarks on the first European hip-hop tour.

1988 Hip-hop music annual record sales reaches $100 million.

1970s Graffiti artist Vic pioneers tagging on subway trains in New York City.

1984 *Graffiti Rock*, the first hip-hop television program, premieres.

1993 Rapper Snoop Dogg's album *Doggystyle* is the first debut album to hit the music charts at number one.

2006 Queen Latifah becomes the first hip-hop artist to receive a star on the Hollywood Walk of Fame.

1989 DJ Jazzy Jeff & The Fresh Prince become the first hip-hop artists to win a Grammy Award.

2003 Rapper Eminem becomes the first hip-hop artist to win an Academy Award.

2005 Hip-hop artist Kanye West appears on the cover of *Time* magazine.

1989 Rap is added as a new category to the *Billboard* charts.

1997 East Coast rapper Notorious B.I.G. (aka Biggie Smalls) is murdered.

2004 First National Hip-Hop Political Convention is held in Newark, New Jersey.

1989 — **2000** — **2006**

1990s Hip-hop emerges in Europe.

1996 West Coast rapper Tupac Shakur is shot and killed.

2005 Rapper Will Smith opens the Philadelphia Live 8 concert as part of 10 simultaneous concerts held worldwide to bring attention to the extreme poverty in Africa.

1989 First gangsta rap album, *Straight Outta Compton*, is released by N.W.A.

2001 The hip-hop political action group, Hip-Hop Summit Action Network, is founded by Russell Simmons.

1992 Dr. Dre's album *The Chronic* is released; it redefines West Coast rap.

2006 The Smithsonian Institute National Museum of American History announces the creation of a new hip-hop exhibition scheduled to open in three to five years.

When Pharrell was asked to speak to the Oxford Union, he ventured where few had gone before, let alone hip-hop stars. His appearance proves how far hip-hop—and Pharrell Williams—has come in the world of mainstream music.

1

Pharrell Goes to Oxford

Oxford University, with its ivy-covered walls and centuries-old traditions, may not seem a likely place to find an American hip-hop star. But that's exactly where Pharrell Williams was on November 22, 2004, speaking to the Oxford Union. In his speech, he described the importance of music: "In my eyes, life is one big movie, and music is the soundtrack to our lives."

Speaking to the Oxford Union was a high honor, one that few people are invited to perform. The Union is one of the best-known and most **exclusive** debating societies in the world. A number of statesmen and prime ministers have cut their **oratory** teeth deliberating on the Union's floor. The society has also throughout its history been revered—at least by its members—as nearly hallowed ground, where freedom of speech reigns. British prime minister Harold MacMillan once referred to the society as "the last **bastion** of free speech in the Western world." To be invited as a guest speaker to such a prestigious institution shows how far

Pharrell Williams (sometimes called Skateboard P) has come in his music career—and it demonstrates the respect he has earned.

Music has always been an important part of Pharrell Williams's life, and he believes it is an important part of all people's lives—whether they realize it or not. He went on in his speech to the Oxford Union to say:

> **"There's something magical about a rhythm you've never heard before. No matter where you are, whatever galaxy, where there's life there's movement. And where there's movement there's sound. And where there's sound, there's music."**

The Man Behind the Curtain

Pharrell Williams is not your typical hip-hop star. He did not earn his fame scratching records as a **DJ** or spitting rhymes as an **MC**, although he has done both. Instead, he is most famous for his work as a **producer**; as part of the production duo the Neptunes, he is one of the most influential forces in the hip-hop and pop music worlds.

Along with his Neptunes partner, Chad Hugo, Pharrell Williams has been the brains behind hits for Justin Timberlake, Snoop Dogg, Mariah Carey, Janet Jackson, Nelly, Gwen Stefani, Busta Rhymes, Britney Spears, and many more. But Pharrell doesn't just create hits for others. Being a successful producer has opened the music industry's doors to Pharrell, allowing him to launch a solo career. In recent years, his own singles have begun moving up the charts.

Pharrell's music could be described as eclectic; in other words, it features many different styles from many different eras. Listening to music Pharrell has produced or performed, one may hear pop, **R&B**, or rock. His music is modern, sometimes even groundbreaking, but it can also carry echoes of the 1990s and '80s. The genre that Pharrell primarily works in, however, is hip-hop, a musical tradition that has its roots in the 1960s and '70s.

Hip-Hop: Born in the Bronx

Hip-hop is an urban cultural movement defined by music, art, and dance that began in the 1970s in the Bronx, New York. At that time, the African American and Latino communities there began experimenting

Long before Pharrell made a name for himself as a performer, he and producing partner, Chad Hugo, were behind some of the biggest names on the music scene. Here, Chad and Pharrell join Justin Timberlake (right) for the 2003 MTV Video Music Awards.

During hip-hop's early days, b-boys performed in clubs around New York City. Before long, these talented break-dancers moved their exhibitions to the city's street corners, where everyone could watch them move their bodies in ways that seemed almost impossible.

with new ways of expressing themselves and critiquing their often-harsh world. This expression manifested itself in a new form of music called hip-hop or rap, art called graffiti or tagging, and dance called b-boying or break dancing.

The hip-hop cultural revolution was a young people's movement, fought in public spaces. Visually, individuals and groups created an art form by tagging the places they had been or the terrain they claimed; their graffiti was painted on buildings, buses, bridges, and other public structures. Musically, rapping and b-boying filled the streets and parks with rhythm. There, young men used their voices and bodies to do battle for respect and territory.

Today, we think of gangs battling with guns, but in the 1970s, rap and break dancing became ways for young men to show their skills, "fight" their opponents, and gain followers. Unfortunately, however, rapping and dancing did not replace violence in the streets. But these forms of creative expression became vital parts of street culture and gave birth to what we know as hip-hop. Today, hip-hop culture is influential all over the world and can be seen not only in the popular music that defines it, but also in the fashion, language, and other cultural elements it has inspired.

The Anatomy of Hip-Hop Music

Hip-hop music is unique in the musical world, perhaps most notably because it does not use traditional musicians or instruments. In fact, when hip-hop was first developed, it did not use "original" musical scores at all, and much hip-hop still does not today. Instead, the music of hip-hop was created by a DJ using songs that already existed. An MC, who raps to the music the DJ creates, accompanies the DJ.

To create the music, the DJ isolates a song's breaks, the portions of the music that contain the beat. Originally, these breaks were isolated from **funk** and **disco** songs, but today they are also taken from rock, **soul**, and other hip-hop songs. The DJ then takes the isolated breaks, usually two, and plays them simultaneously, manipulating them to create a new sound. Traditionally, this is done using two turntables (a record on each turntable) and basic equipment including a **mixer**, amplifier, and speakers.

In the early days of hip-hop, the DJs were the stars of the music. Their practice of isolating breaks and turntabling has its roots in Jamaican music; it developed further in New York City clubs and at block parties. At these venues, the goal was to keep the partygoers dancing, and the DJs knew the breaks were the most danceable parts of the songs. By isolating the breaks and keeping them playing, the audience could continue dancing uninterrupted. A good DJ was much appreciated and respected by the audience.

The DJ's role has changed over the years. Hip-hop songs are now created in studios and played over the radio. Having a good DJ at a club is still important, but technology has changed much about the creation and playing of hip-hop music. Today much of the hip-hop music, especially "pop hip-hop," uses instrumentals and **synthesizers** to create the beats rather than isolating the breaks of existing songs, and the role of the live DJ is greatly diminished.

The focus of today's hip-hop music is on the MC. In the early days of hip-hop, MCs had a secondary role; they introduced the DJ and kept the crowd entertained during breaks between songs. But the MCs quickly expanded their position, adding jokes, commentary, and ultimately delivering beat-driven performances. Their crowd-pleasing phrasing melded with the music and became increasingly elaborate. The use of rhyme became a focal point of the MC's performance, and what emerged was known as rapping. Rapping usually consists not only of rhyming, but also of assonance—the repeated use of vowel sounds—and alliteration—using a string of words that all begin with the same consonant.

Beatboxing, creating drum- and bass-like beats using only the human voice, is also an important aspect of hip-hop music. A skilled beatboxer can provide the entire percussion portion of a song using no other instrument than a set of vocal chords. A group of beatboxers providing the music for a skilled MC's rhymes creates a sound like no other. Beatboxing faded from prominence for many years, but it is currently enjoying a revival in urban music the world over.

Hip-Hop in Mainstream America

Hip-hop has come a long way from its rebellious urban roots. Although it still has much of the same spirit of the original urban movement, hip-hop is now definitely part of the mainstream music world. It's also a cash cow for music executives. In an interview with VH1, Pharrell Williams stated:

> **"Now hip-hop has become big business. People use the same marketing strategies that they use on toilet tissue and candy bars for marketing videos and songs. Those corporate dudes realized how much money was in it. Did you ever think you'd see the day when hip-hop actually sold more than Barbra Streisand? Even when [stars like Streisand] put their greatest hits out, they might get No. 1 for the first week, but Eminem gonna come and slaughter you the next week."**

DJs and their turntables were the stars of early hip-hop. Their scratching and mixing talents made some very famous. Though DJs' role has changed, they were responsible in hip-hop's early days for getting people onto the dance floor.

Some people think that as hip-hop has become popularized and mainstreamed, it has been weakened, watered down, made less cutting edge. Pharrell Williams agrees that much of the music is now produced just to sell records, and that this can cause producers and artists to become **formulaic** rather than **innovative**. But he disagrees that hip-hop's mainstream popularity is overall a bad thing. He believes that as more people in America are exposed to hip-hop, they will begin to understand the world hip-hop came from: the world of urban poverty and prejudice.

Besides his musical talents, Pharrell has become a spokesman for the hip-hop movement. He often speaks of his hope that as hip-hop moves into the mainstream, people will begin to understand its roots: poverty and prejudice.

Although hip-hop began in black communities, Pharrell believes that a white rapper actually has much to do with hip-hop's increased appeal in mainstream America. That rapper is Eminem. Williams told VH1:

"He was our middle finger to the corporates. Those corporate guys didn't really care for us too much, but Eminem was like their own son letting you know that he loves hip-hop. Now you have to recant everything you've ever said, because hip-hop is your children and suburbia America. It's gotten to where you've got Republicans saying they liked *8 Mile*. They're now hearing us. Eminem, thank you sir. You've made them hate you, and now they love you, and I love it. You're doing a great service to hip-hop right now."

Another person doing a great service for hip-hop—and for music in general—is Pharrell himself. He's committed to making incredible music that affects peoples' lives and touches their souls. He says the trick to making music is "to make it undeniable, make it speak to your spirit and everybody else's. Hopefully it does what it's supposed to do." Pharrell Williams' music is clearly doing what it's supposed to do, touching people's lives and creating fans the world over.

Given his background, Pharrell wasn't expected to achieve great things. Who would have known that the young man shown in this 1991 high school yearbook photo would become a star and a starmaker—and a fashion icon?

2

Musical Roots

When Pharrell Williams gave his speech to the Oxford Union, he joined an exclusive list of people who have performed this honor. The list includes famous names such as Winston Churchill, the Dalai Lama, Malcolm X, Robert Kennedy, Clint Eastwood, and Michael Jackson—impressive company for a young man who wasn't expected to go far.

Pharrell Williams was born in Virginia Beach, Virginia, on April 4, 1973, to Pharaoh and Carolyn Williams. He is the oldest of three boys. His younger brothers are Cato (who is ten years younger than Pharrell and is now a professional skateboarder) and Solomon (who is twenty years younger than Pharrell). He also has two half brothers—Pharaoh and David.

A Hard Life in Virginia

Few people expected Pharrell, or any of the young people where he lived, to become successful in life, and no one expected them to become music stars. In the area where he grew up, more kids joined gangs than went to college, and many would die as young adults, victims of the violence that gangs bred. After his speech to the Oxford Union, Pharrell said,

> **"You have to understand that the world I grew up in was not one of high expectations. No one told us when we were young to be ambitious. In Virginia, if you didn't die in your twenties, you'd probably end up in prison or live a life of drugs. I feel so privileged that I've been blessed by God. I feel mega, mega fortunate."**

But growing up in the South wasn't all bad. There was always music, something that was important to Pharrell's life even as a very young child. When Pharrell was seven years old, his family moved, leaving the inner city behind for the calmer, safer-seeming suburbs. Pharrell remembers that the music from this time in his life came from very different sources, and he believes this is partially responsible for his tendency to mix different musical forms in his work today. In an interview with hitz.fm, he recalled:

> **"We lived across the street from a biker group called The Renegades, which were like Hell's Angels. They played a lot of rock 'n' roll, so they'd be playing "Born to Be Wild" across the street. Meanwhile in my house, my mom and dad are playing Earth, Wind & Fire, but on the radio they are playing Rick James and Queen. I never really lost that."**

Growing up in Virginia may have been tough, but it formed Pharrell as a person and as an artist. His childhood experiences in Virginia gave him musical roots. Growing up in the South also exposed Pharrell to some of the most important people in his life, people without whom he might never have had a musical career at all.

A Friend for Life

One of the most important people in Pharrell's life is his friend Chad Hugo, also a Virginia Beach native. The pair met while still in school. Although they attended different schools, they both participated in

Pharrell and Chad Hugo (seen here in a 2003 photo) have been friends since their high school days. Their friendship would grow into possibly music's most successful—critically and financially—business relationship, as well as into a musical group.

an **improvisational** music program. Pharrell played drums in the program, and Chad played the saxophone. The boys quickly realized they shared both a love of music and talent. Eventually that friendship would grow to be one of the most successful partnerships in the music industry.

In a joint interview with VH1, in which Pharrell and Chad discussed their friendship and business relationship, Chad recalled that in their childhood they would

> **" . . . bang on the cafeteria tables. [Pharrell] would freestyle. That developed into making music in my garage after school. [Pharrell] would come up with hooks and beats. We had the cheapest keyboards ever, like a small Casio. . . . When we started working together, Pharrell would bring to my house records that his parents listened to. You'd have a loop of some guy singing with all these instruments and orchestration behind it. We'd listen to it over and over again, then turn it off and mix something inspired by its sound. That's not a formula. We just did that."**

Pharrell's friendship with Chad grew; they formed their first band when they were still in grade school. The band was called Nobody Knows. Eventually, they would rename their partnership the Neptunes. Not many childhood friendships last into adulthood, let alone grow into successful business partnerships, but Pharrell and Chad are still together, and the Neptunes is the name by which they are still known today.

Making the Music

As a teenager, Pharrell attended Princess Anne High School in Virginia Beach. **Serendipitously**, a record producer, Teddy Riley, opened his studio, Future Records, next door to the school. Teddy Riley had become famous working with artists like Bobby Brown and Al B. Sure. Around the same time that he opened his studio, Pharrell and Chad formed a hip-hop group called SBI, which stood for Surrounded By Idiots. The other member of the group was Timbaland. Today, Timbaland has also risen to be one of the most successful, influential, and sought-after producers in the hip-hop industry.

A talent show performance led to a huge break for Pharrell. In the audience was the hot record producer Teddy Riley (here with Denise Rich). He immediately recognized Pharrell's talent and asked him to write some lyrics. It was Pharrell's first professional music gig.

While still in high school, Pharrell and Chad performed in a talent show that would change their lives. Riley happened to attend and recognized the boys' talent. He enlisted Pharrell to write some lyrics. Pharrell's first professional work in the music industry was a bigger success than many people have in a whole lifetime. Pharrell wrote the rap verse for Wrecks-N-Effect's single "Rump Shaker." The single went double **platinum**.

After that, Pharrell got more offers for writing lines, making beats, mixing music, and eventually singing chorus and background vocals. Nevertheless, for years his work was relatively sparse, and he was by no means a force in the music industry.

Not Hip Enough?

Despite his early opportunities, it was not easy for Pharrell to break into the music business. His co-Neptune, Chad Hugo recalled in an interview with VH1 that lots of people felt Pharrell and Chad didn't have the right image for this highly image-oriented industry. But the young men never let other people's opinions get in their way. Pharrell

Together, Pharrell and Chad—the Neptunes—had early success, but maintaining that success wasn't easy. Critics claimed they didn't project the right image for hip-hop. The two couldn't be deterred, however, and they continued to work in their own way.

and Chad knew they could make music that would make people respond emotionally, so they kept working toward their goal. Hugo said of that time period:

> **❝You have people who are like, 'Who are these nerdy dudes?' At the end of the day, your music speaks for itself. Three years ago when we did a video, I had on like cowboy boots, regular jeans, and a polo shirt. My hair was big and matted and I didn't care. I had people thinking I was an engineer. When we would walk in the studio they would be asking me where to order the best pizza. I'm like 'Dog, I don't know, man. Let me fix up this track here.' I guess they're not used to seeing an Asian making music. But I'm just here to get people's heads bobbing.❞**

In the late 1990s, things began to change. In 1998, N.O.R.E.'s "Superthug" was burning up the charts, and Pharrell and Chad had produced the song. For the first time, listeners of urban radio and pop began to recognize the name Neptunes. Before long, Americans would be hearing a lot more of the dynamic duo, and those who had doubted the Neptunes could no longer deny the innovative sounds they created. For the first time, the music they produced began to climb the charts.

As part of the Neptunes, Pharrell got more work, especially work that featured his lyrical and singing abilities. Not only did he have more opportunities coming his way, but the stars for whom he produced were getting bigger as well. Soon the biggest names in hip-hop wanted Pharrell and Chad working on their albums. The Neptunes were on the rise, and within a few years, they were some of the most sought-after producers in the music industry. The Neptunes were finally steaming ahead on their mission: to change the music world.

When Pharrell moved behind the mic to sing background vocals and choruses for the artists the Neptunes produced, the public paid attention to his smooth, captivating voice, and his good looks. He was developing a fan base, even without a song of his own.

3

Changing Pop Music

Being a producer is very much behind-the-scenes work. You can't expect to earn the fans that musicians and singers have. Generally, you can't even expect people to recognize your name. Certainly no one is going to flag you down on the street to get your autograph . . . unless you happen to be a producer named Pharrell Williams.

In the late 1990s, as the Neptunes produced ever-bigger hits with ever-bigger stars, Pharrell began to move from behind the glass of the recording studio out into the public eye. It started with singing some background vocals, then performing the choruses for other stars' songs. After a while, he began appearing in the music videos of songs that featured his voice. Before long, his good looks, smooth voice, and quiet-yet-confident presence were stealing the show. Unlike most producers, Pharrell Williams, who had never released his own album or even his own single, had his own fans.

Innovators in the Industry

Critics couldn't deny that there was something undeniably special about the music the Neptunes produced. Soon their influence spilled over from urban, hip-hop radio into the world of pop.

In 2001, Britney Spears was performing her hit single "I'm a Slave for U" on MTV's Video Music Awards—but Pharrell Williams was the one savoring the moment. After all, he was the one responsible for writing the song, and he and Chad Hugo had produced it. Pop superstar Britney Spears may have been singing it, but it was *their* song.

In an interview, Pharrell talked about watching Britney on stage, and how the success of the song made him feel. He said that at that moment, it didn't matter how critics received the song, how Britney Spears performed it, or even if the audience liked it. What mattered to him was seeing his song, his lyrics, performed by a major star at a major venue. For Pharrell, it was confirmation that he had succeeded in the music industry. The doors were finally open. All he had to do was walk through. He told VH1:

> **❝ ['I'm a Slave for U'] wasn't just our production. Those were my lyrics and everything. I didn't care if she flopped at the show; that was my moment. I didn't care if everybody in the place hated it. We made it. Pop-wise, what little girl doesn't know Britney Spears? ❞**

Besides Britney Spears, the Neptunes were now producing for famous hip-hop and pop stars, including Jay-Z, Usher, Busta Rhymes, Justin Timberlake, and No Doubt. Hip-hop and pop weren't the only types of music Pharrell Williams wished to change, however. He was also deeply committed to R&B. In a 2001 interview, he spoke to fans about his intentions:

> **❝ I want you to raise your awareness and listen to this R&B. When I tell you I'm gonna reshape it, I'm gonna get rid of this Range Rover R&B and all this 'platinum' and 'Bentleys' talk. There's so much more to black life and culture than the materialistic portion that seems to consume all the lyrical content on the radio. I want to offer our difference and perspective, and I promise we're gonna make people move and feel R&B again. ❞**

Every time fans hear Britney Spears sing "I'm a Slave for U," they have Pharrell to thank. He wrote the song, and he and Chad produced it. Britney Spears is just one of many stars who have found success with Pharrell's music.

Pharrell's words reflect his deepest feeling about music: that the focus of music shouldn't be on fame, money, stars, **paparazzi**, and **bling**. Music is about life, culture, soul, and touching people's hearts and minds. R&B, soul, hip-hop, and pop music all offer opportunities to extend people's awareness, to give them a glimpse into other worlds besides their own, to help them understand the challenges and triumphs experienced by the people in America who have often lacked a voice.

In 2002, Pharrell Williams received confirmation of what by now most people already knew: the Neptunes were a force with which to

As the Neptunes' reputation grew on the music scene, bigger and bigger stars sought out the talented duo to use their magic on their CDs and singles. One who came knocking was one of the biggest names ever in hip-hop, the legendary Jay-Z.

be reckoned in the music industry. The confirmation came in the form of awards. In August, the Neptunes received the Producer of the Year Award at the Source Awards, and then in December, they were honored again with the Producers of the Year Award at the Billboard Music Awards.

Becoming N.E.R.D.

Before long, Pharrell and Chad decided that producing music for other artists wasn't going to be enough for them: they wanted to create music of their own as well. To do so, they tapped into another musical genre—rock. Together with their childhood friend, Shay Hayley, Pharrell and Chad formed a band called N.E.R.D. N.E.R.D.'s music draws from many different styles, including hip-hop and soul, but the band is generally referred to as an "alternative rock" group. On their Web site, the band members describe their group in the following way:

Producing wasn't enough for Pharrell and Chad. They wanted more of the music scene. So Shay (left) joined the pair, and they became N.E.R.D.—No One Ever Really Dies. Their first album, *In Search Of*, went gold.

> **"N.E.R.D. is the offspring of the Neptunes id, a fly-or-die, thrash-around, do-as-you-will, set-your-soul-on-fire alter-ego that subscribes to no rules, adheres to no agenda. It is Pharrell, Chad and Shay—a trio whose chemistry allows the uninhibited exploration of the sounds, emotions and impulses of self and society, of identity and belonging. Of life."**

There is some heavy philosophy behind the band's name. On the band's Web site, Pharrell explains the beliefs behind the name:

> **"N.E.R.D. stands for No One Ever Really Dies. The Neptunes are who we are and N.E.R.D. is what we do. It's our life. N.E.R.D. is just a basic belief, man. People's energies are made of their souls. When you die, that energy may disperse but it isn't destroyed. Energy cannot be destroyed. It can manifest in a different way, but even then it's like their souls are going somewhere. If it's going to heaven or hell or even if it's going into a fog or somewhere in the atmosphere to lurk unbeknownst to itself, it's going somewhere."**

In 2001, N.E.R.D. put out its first album, *In Search Of.* The album was released first in Europe. Then, feeling that the music needed more work, the band teamed up with the funk-rock band Spymob and re-recorded the album before it was released worldwide in 2002. *In Search Of* reached a respectable number fifty-nine on the U.S. *Billboard* 200 album chart—a list of the highest selling albums in the United States— and some of the singles made it onto the top-40 charts. The album also won the Shortlist Music Prize, an award given to the best album of the year that hasn't gone gold at the time of the nominations. The album did later go gold, selling over 500,000 copies.

The Next Big Risk

Pharrell Williams was now part of the most sought-after production team in the music industry, and the lead singer of a successful rock group as well. For many artists, this would be as far as they dared to go. To venture out on one's own after being part of a successful collaboration or band is a huge risk. Many artists fail when they try to establish solo careers after making it big in partnerships. But Pharrell always wants to be moving ahead, breaking down barriers, and trying something new—risky or not.

In 2003, Pharrell embarked on a solo music career with the release of his first single "Frontin.'" The song features Jay-Z and was a huge hit on urban radio and a big summer hit on popular radio as well. *Billboard* magazine later ranked "Frontin'" as the thirty-fourth largest hit of the year. Pharrell-love was "in," and the Neptunes took advantage of this period of good will by releasing their own **debut** album.

Although the production team had produced countless songs for countless artists, they had never yet released an album on their

In 2003, Pharrell began a solo career with megahit "Frontin'," and he was on his way. But his producing days weren't over. In 2004, the Neptunes won the Non-classical Producer of the Year Grammy. Here he is (fourth from left) after announcing the Grammy nominees.

own. Riding on the wave of Pharrell's recent success, they release *The Neptunes Presents . . . Clones.* The album debuted at number one on the *Billboard* 200 album chart and eventually went gold.

Becoming the Musicians

In 2004, riding high on the wave of Pharrell Williams's success, N.E.R.D. released its second album, this one titled *Fly or Die.* In an interview with VH1, Pharrell spoke of the album's title and the reasons for the name. As with much of what Pharrell does, there's some serious philosophy behind the words. He said:

> **❝ *Fly or Die* is the only choice an eagle's egg hatching in midair that fell out of its mother's nest would have. The only choice you really have in life is to fly or die. I felt [the title] for so many reasons. That's where the world was [when we named the album]. We're either gonna fly together or die together. For me, in my relentless pursuit of love, it's either fly or die; be optimistic or wither away into nothing. That should be everybody's motto in life. Go for it. If you don't go for it, you're gonna lose it. ❞**

On the band's Web site, Chad Hugo weighs in on the album's musical and lyrical depth. He says,

> **❝ It's evolution, for real. There's an entire dimension to music and life that we touched on with *In Search Of . . . ,* but that was only the beginning. Those were only doors to this other dimension and with this album we are there. . . . I think we learned a lot from the first album, and we've opened up more here. I think we're going places we haven't gone before. ❞**

Fly or Die performed better than *In Search Of,* breaking the top ten on the *Billboard* 200. *Fly or Die* also went gold, selling more than 500,000 copies. For the album, in the spirit of Pharrell's "go for it, fly-or-die" approach, the band tried something new and risky for them. They decided to play their own instruments live. Pharrell has played drums since childhood, so in a way, being a musician is not new to him.

Fly or Die, N.E.R.D.'s second album, came out in 2004. It was even more successful than their debut album. It was also the first time the group played their own instruments live, although each is an accomplished musician.

However, performing live as a musician in the recording studio and on the stage is different. It was a big step for artists who do most of their producing using synthesizers and digital sound equipment. On their Web site, Chad talks about the challenge:

Pharrell performs live at an event to promote N.E.R.D.'s album *Fly or Die*. Being part of N.E.R.D. gave Pharrell the chance to show the more "quirky" side of his personality, and the fans approved.

"We've always played our own instruments in everything we do, but we convert them into programming for the final tracks. For *Fly or Die*, we decided to pick up the instruments and play ourselves and leave it like that. It's more honest, and people don't know this side to us yet."

Pharrell also likes working with N.E.R.D. because it allows him to be honest with his personality. His bandmates comment on this situation on their Web site as well. Chad says, "[Pharrell is] more quirky in real life than he is in videos and other people's songs." Shay agrees and adds, "[Pharrell's] a little more eccentric in his personality and in N.E.R.D. he can pull that off."

Pharrell's willingness to be his real self, to expose his unique quirkiness, took courage—but his fans responded. Pharrell refused to play it safe. And his daring made him a star.

Pharrell's fame wasn't bound by the borders of the United States. His talents—as a producer and as a performer—brought him recognition and fans all over the world. In 2005, he performed with Japanese rappers in Tokyo.

4

Stardom

Pharrell Williams was now a world-famous producer, a member of a band that had created two gold albums, a familiar voice in songs all over urban and pop radio, and a familiar face in music videos. But one thing was still missing. He had success that many artists only dream of, but he still did not have his own solo album.

Pharrell's fans wanted more, and so in 2005, Pharrell set out to give them what they wanted. That September, he released his single "Can I Have It Like That." The song featured Gwen Stefani and was to be the opening track on his debut album, *In My Mind*. The song was a huge success, and Pharrell and Gwen Stefani were the perfect musical pair. The hit song generated many new Pharrell fans and put everyone in the mood for more. To make the most of the positive publicity "Can I Have It Like That" generated, Pharrell's album was planned for release shortly after the single hit the airwaves. However, not everything worked out as planned.

Setbacks on the Solo Road

Pharrell's first solo album, *In My Mind*, was originally due to be released in November 2005. Then the date got pushed back to December. Just before the release, however, Pharrell pulled back again. A bit of a **perfectionist**, he decided there was still more work he wanted to do before releasing his debut album into the world. To his fans' disappointment, he moved the release date to July 2006, but promised the album would be worth the wait. He told fans that *In My Mind* would allow them to look inside and see the real Pharrell. The album would consist of fourteen songs, seven hip-hop and seven R&B. Pharrell explained, "The hip-hop songs are more the **introspective** side of my view and how I look at life, and the R&B stuff is the more vulnerable side."

Pharrell's Neptunes partner, Chad Hugo, harbors no ill feelings toward his friend for going solo. After all, together they are still the Neptunes. Furthermore, Chad said he's been very moved watching Pharrell create his music and build his solo career. In an interview with htz.fm, he commented on *In My Mind* and how listening to it has made him feel:

> **"We came from a small town, which makes you kinda go through a lot. Virginia is sorta like this nine-to-five town [and] our parents probably didn't even expect us to take our music this far. . . . [We] started out at band camp, and we thought that was going to be it after a while. But we took that love and applied it, and I think his message is that you could do it too. And that's how I feel when I listen to his stuff."**

Finding the Time

With a successful career with the Neptunes, it wasn't easy for Pharrell to find the time to create his own work. His solo career has been built piece by piece whenever Pharrell can find a moment. In an interview with MTV, he described how he found the time to work on *In My Mind.* "When I'm in the studio working on different people's sessions, in between sessions and before they get there, I work on tracks. That's how I do my [songs]."

This is how Pharrell enlisted Gwen Stefani to be on his hit song "Can I Have It Like That." At the time, Williams was producing for

While working on his debut album, Pharrell also worked with Gwen Stefani on a new project. So enthusiastic was she about his album, she stopped working on her song to record Pharrell's "Can I Have It Like That?"

Stefani, and they were in the recording studio working on Stefani's song "Breaking Up." Williams mentioned that he was working on a new song and hoped Stefani would be on it. She said she wanted to hear the song, and she liked it so much that she insisted they stop working on "Breaking Up" and spend the rest of the recording session working on Pharrell's song.

For Pharrell, working with Gwen Stefani was a perfect match. Both prefer to create their own style, and neither cares much about what other people think. He told MTV:

> **"I think me and Gwen are like the same people. We're people cut from their own cloth. Not a different cloth, their own cloth. Gwen is like the girl in high school who had her own style. Everyone went to high school with that girl, and she's cute with it. And then you got the other girls with the purple hair, standing by the lockers, who are just followers of a musical movement. Gwen marches to the beat of her own drum. We wave that flag together, 'Just be you, who cares?'"**

In a separate interview with VH1, Gwen Stefani returned the compliment, saying of Williams, "We have an incredible chemistry. He has so many sides to him. He's so talented; he's so inspiring. I feel lucky to know him and be able to work with him."

A New Level of Fame

Stepping into the limelight has been a new experience for Pharrell, who had been more accustomed to being behind the scenes. Working alongside mega pop stars has shown him some of the more difficult side of fame. For example, in spring 2006, he shot a music video in Paris with Mariah Carey for her song "Say Somethin.'" In one of the scenes, Williams and Carey play a superstar couple trying to escape from the paparazzi. Actors were hired to play paparazzi in the scene, but as Williams and Carey later explained in an interview, there would have been no need to fake it. The set was crawling with so many real members of the paparazzi that there wouldn't have been any need for the actors at all. Pharrell commented on the experience to VH1:

> **"That's just a regular day in the life for Mariah, probably. I'm a low-key guy, so there's no paparazzi under the studio console, or in my apartment, or jumping out of my pool. I'm just not into it. So it's weird when you have these people running up, especially in Paris—they're on Vespas, doing wheelies, and it's wild."**

Despite the paparazzi, Pharrell is happy to have achieved everything he's achieved. Not everyone thought he could do it. Many people told Pharrell he didn't have the right image to be a solo hip-hop star. Today, Pharrell delights in having proved them wrong. He told MTV, "It's

In 2006, Pharrell performed with superstar Mariah Carey in her music video for "Say Somethin'." This experience introduced Pharrell to a new level of fame. Photographers followed them everywhere, and almost immediately, rumors began to fly that they were a couple.

absolutely bitter, because when I wanted to get in the game they was like, 'You dress funny.' I kind of rub it in the faces of the naysayers."

A New Title

In 2005, Pharrell also received **accolades** of a totally different kind. Having already been recognized for his skills as a producer and hip-hop artist, now he was being recognized for his fashion sense, which was so

The Rise of the Freedom Tower

REBUILDING AT GROUND ZERO.
THE EPIC STRUGGLE BEGINS (PART 1).

An Esquire Exclusive

Esquire

SEPTEMBER
2005

The
Best
Dressed
List

21 Style Icons
ON WHAT TO WEAR &
HOW TO WEAR IT

JOSH LUCAS,
PHARRELL WILLIAMS,
AND LUKE WILSON

Plus:
SEND YOUR CHORES
TO BANGALORE:
HOW I OUTSOURCED
MY LIFE, BY A.J. JACOBS

Talented, good looking, and stylin': that certainly sums up Pharrell Williams, and the editors at *Esquire* couldn't agree more. His style philosophy of "comfort and flow" led to his being named 2005's Best Dressed Man in the World.

good that *Esquire* magazine named him 2005's Best Dressed Man in the World. The title is quite an honor; Pharrell came out on top of the world's other most fashionable men, among them George Clooney, Donald Trump, UN Secretary-General Kofi Annan, Japanese prime minister Junichiro Koizumi, former president Bill Clinton, and fellow rapper Jay-Z.

Nick Sullivan, the fashion editor of *Esquire*, said the list featured, "the most innovative, never-trendy, and always perfectly clad-for-the-occasion individuals who roam the globe as walking examples of what it means to be a man well-clothed." Pharrell doesn't take the title too seriously, however. In an interview with MTV, he said:

> **"It's about comfort and flow. It's never about whether I'm the best-dressed guy in the room. I never go, 'Oh, I'm killin' 'em tonight!' Things just need to fit naturally. Fashion's more about feel than science."**

Whether Pharrell takes his world title seriously or not, however, it's a nice response to all those who said he "dressed funny" and didn't have the right image to be a hip-hop star.

Pharrell's individual success hasn't meant the end of the Neptunes as record producers. Their business continues to grow and now includes a record label. One of their biggest artists is Snoop Dogg, shown here with Pharrell in 2004 at the Brit Awards.

5

Beyond the Music

For those fans who can't get enough of Pharrell Williams, there are now many more ways to enjoy his artistry and style. Being a superstar producer and musician has led to countless opportunities, and now Pharrell has his own record label, his own movies, his own clothing line, even his own line of footwear.

The Neptunes, along with their manager, Rob Walker, started their own record label, Star Trak. Today, a number of important artists, including Snoop Dogg, Slim Thug, Clipse, Fam-Lay, Rasco P. Coldchain, and Vanessa Marquez are signed with the label. Pharrell also produces his solo work with Star Trak, and N.E.R.D. is signed with the company as well.

Pharrell has always believed it's important for artists to be informed and involved in the business side of things, and that was part of the reason for creating Star Trak. In an interview he talked about the dangers of being a musician who is powerless on the production side. He described to VH1 the situation faced by many artists:

"Let's say you get a million dollar deal. Of your full advance the government's taking half [in taxes]. So right then and there it's only a half a million dollars. That million dollars you gotta recoup. Recouping with the amount that they give you is like trying to fill up a bucket from a barrel with a spoon. Yeah, there's a barrel of water that's been earned in terms of your CD sales, but you're only rationed a teaspoonful. It's gonna take a lot of barrels in order for you to make one little bucket, because all you have is a spoon to recoup with."

For Pharrell, managing a record label, particularly a record label with which he is signed, is just good business. It's a way to ensure that he and other artists, the people actually creating the music, aren't left out in the cold when the music starts to sell.

A Movie Star?

Managing a record label, however, is just one of the spin-off opportunities Pharrell has had since becoming successful in the music world. Another opportunity has been in movie production. In 2003, Pharrell and Chad released a straight-to-video movie titled, *The Neptunes Presents . . . Dude, We're Going to Rio*. Not ones to take themselves too seriously, the movie is a lighthearted story of a young man hopelessly chasing love. Pharrell described the movie to VH1:

"It's unscripted, un-everything. It's a walk into our funny, hilarious, ridiculous, stupid, retarded, mindless, insane lives. It's a very candid, sincere perception of us. It's just something for Neptunes fans to go out and buy and see us be stupid. It's really improvisational."

He went on to say that one reason for making the movie was that he didn't "want to bore people. I want to provide different experiences. If I just put out records all the time, it'd be boring. This is a fun movie, just a few days of our lives, man."

Dude, We're Going to Rio may have been all fun and games, but in 2004, Pharrell decided to cut his serious-acting teeth in a short film called *The Ecology of Love*. In the film, which runs just eighteen minutes, Pharrell plays the lead role of Andre, an actor in search of meaning and soul. Pharrell plans to do more films in the future, and bigger ones. He's currently looking at both the acting and producing side of a number of scripts.

Designer Pharrell

Fans can now get glimpses of Pharrell in movies—and they can also see glimpses of his style on themselves . . . if they would like to purchase Pharrell-designed clothing, that is. There has been much ado about Pharrell's being named the Best Dressed Man in the World, and the title opened a lot of people's eyes to Pharrell's style.

Pharrell is a producer and musician, a movie maker, and has his own clothing and footwear lines. His success in business has not gone unnoticed by others. In 2005, *Black Enterprise* magazine named him one of its Most Powerful Players Under 40.

Now fans can wear Pharrell! In 2005, Pharrell and world-famous Japanese designer Nigo of A Bathing Ape launched the Billionaire Boys Club and Ice Cream clothing lines. Fans of Pharrell's style can buy T-shirts, sweatshirts, and sneakers, among other items.

In 2005, Pharrell teamed with Japanese designer Nigo, of A Bathing Ape, to produce his own clothing lines. One line is Billionaire Boys Club. The other line is Ice Cream. The Billionaire Boys Club line features T-shirts, polos, sweatshirts, jackets, jeans, shorts, and accessories. The Ice Cream line features all these categories, as well as sneakers.

The Meaning of It All

Pharrell Williams, however, doesn't let all of the success of being a producer, musician, label executive, actor, and designer go to his head. He remains ever mindful of how fortunate he has been to have so many opportunities. Most important, he still focuses on the meaning of the music. In an interview with *Remix*, he described his philosophy about his career:

> **"I'm just trying to bring the ammonia back to radio and to television. When I was a kid, you'd run to the screen to see that rapper and the beat was, 'Oh my God.' You'd lose it. I miss that. I appreciate what's going on right now. I appreciate my opportunity. So with my opportunity I'm going to get in. . . . I want to break the color lines . . . that's the way I grew up."**

Furthermore, Pharrell feels that, to survive in the cutthroat music business and stay happy, one must always be mindful that there is more to life than seeking fame and fortune. He believes you must always remember *why* you are striving for the success. He doesn't think people should seek fame and fortune just for fame and fortune's sake; there should be meaning behind what they want to achieve. In an interview with VH1, he explained his thoughts this way:

> **"You have to be secure yourself and know that you will be a good provider for whoever is involved in your life. When you're a musician, there's more to your life than just your music. Chad was fortunate enough to meet his wife years ago and have two beautiful children. I haven't been as fortunate, but there's more to a musician's life than music—family members, friends, things happening, things not happening."**

Pharrell the Activist

Many celebrities say that the greatest thing about achieving fame is that their success puts them in a position to help others by making them influential with the public and bringing them in contact with powerful people. Like many stars, Pharrell Williams is using his fame for **activism**, trying to make the world a better place.

Pharrell is concerned with many other issues besides music, including politics. In the 2004 presidential election, he did a broadcast with P. Diddy, encouraging people to get out and vote. In an interview with the BBC, he wasn't shy about sharing his political views. Concerning the outcome of the election, he said:

> **"I'm not happy because most of the people I've spoken to aren't. There's more minorities in the States than there are a majority, and there were more people who needed Kerry than those who needed Bush. When I did a broadcast with P. Diddy encouraging people to vote, I thought how it was the pimps, prostitutes, and drug addicts who needed to vote more than those out in the suburbs."**

Pharrell's activism isn't just in the political sphere. He's also concerned with the treatment of animals. In 2004, he supported PETA—People for the Ethical Treatment of Animals—by lending his voice for an answering-machine message. The message was available for people to download from peta2.com, and it stated, "The person you're leaving this message for wants you to check out peta2.com and be kind to animals—and so do we."

Advice for the Next Generation

In an interview with VH1, Pharrell also offered advice to anyone wanting to get into the music industry. With his experience as both a producer and musician, the advice comes straight from the source. He says that the first thing developing artists must do is be realistic and understand the true nature of the music industry.

> **"It's not platinum and diamonds and Mercedes. It is business, work, concentration, discipline, and understanding. All those other things, they come along with success, and success is derived from educating yourself."**

Pharrell believes it's not only important for young artists to educate themselves about the industry; they must also educate themselves in case their dreams don't come true. Being an industry insider, Pharrell

"STAND UP AND
BE HEARD"
VOTE ON NOVEMBER 2ND

IT'S THAT
SERIOUS!
FOR INFO CONTACT
CITIZENCHANGE.COM
877.381.VOTE

CITIZEN CHANGE

Music and business aren't the only things important to Pharrell. He is also an activist. In 2004, he joined P. Diddy and other musicians in a campaign to get people out to vote. In addition, Pharrell is active with PETA, helping to better the welfare of animals.

has seen firsthand how quickly dreams can be shattered. Furthermore, he knows that it doesn't take just talent to make it; it also takes a good dose of luck. Some of the most talented people in the world have been unable to break into or survive in the music industry, and their experiences should serve as a cautionary tale to others. Pharrell told VH1:

> "Get a degree in something in case this music thing doesn't work out, because it's a vulture-type business. Anybody that wants to get involved with it, do your homework, research it, see what these deals consist of. It's not like you sell two or three million records and

Pharrell Williams has come a long way for someone others thought wouldn't amount to much. He's found success as a musician, a producer, a businessman, and as a person. Through it all, he's never compromised, always staying true to himself.

never work again. You gotta really work hard. When you negotiate your deal, if that company wants you that bad, they'll make some changes."

More than anything else, Pharrell said, it's important to be true to yourself and your art. There will always be someone who wants artists to change their music because they think it will sell better if it's less edgy, less risky, more mainstream, more danceable. But Pharrell believes that to really be successful, you need to recognize when such changes are wise and permissible, and when they alter the core of the message and damage the integrity of the art. Pointing to his head, he said:

"It's what comes from here. It's priceless. The minute you let them put a cheap price on it is when they begin to own you and the way you think. You become insecure and dependent on a system that doesn't give two nothings about you. Don't be afraid to go to school and learn about music. It definitely enables you to do more than what they cookie-cut you out to do. Then learn about the business. Because you don't want to make a good album and then get screwed. It's like doing good all your life but never knowing nothing about the Bible. You don't really have a good chance in heaven, right? Don't do it for nothing, man. Do it for something."

1970s Hip-hop develops in black and Latino neighborhoods of the Bronx, New York City.

1973 Pharrell Williams born on April 4 to Pharaoh and Carolyn Williams in Virginia Beach, Virginia.

1980 Pharrell's family moves from inner city to suburbs of Virginia Beach.

1980s Lifelong friendship develops between Pharrell Williams and Chad Hugo. They will later become the famous production duo, the Neptunes.

1992 Teddy Riley enlists Williams to write a verse for Wrecks-N-Effect's "Rump Shaker." The single goes double platinum.

1998 The Neptunes produce N.O.R.E.'s "Superthug."

2001 The Neptunes produce Britney Spears's "I'm a Slave for U."

N.E.R.D. releases its first album, *In Search Of*, in Europe.

2002 N.E.R.D. releases reworked version of *In Search Of* worldwide. The album goes gold and wins Shortlist Music Prize.

The Neptunes win Producer of the Year awards at the Source Awards and the Billboard Music Awards.

2003 Pharrell releases first solo single, "Frontin'," featuring Jay-Z.

The Neptunes release first album, *The Neptunes Presents . . . Clones*. The album goes gold.

The Neptunes release straight-to-video movie, *The Neptunes Presents . . . Dude, We're Going to Rio*.

2004 N.E.R.D. releases second album, *Fly or Die*. The album goes gold.

Pharrell plays lead role in short film *The Ecology of Love*.

Pharrell does broadcast with P. Diddy encouraging people to vote in the presidential election.

Pharrell supports People for the Ethical Treatment of Animals (PETA) by recording an answering-machine message that people can download from the Internet.

Pharrell Williams gives speech at Oxford Union.

2005 Pharrell is named Best Dressed Man in the World by *Esquire* magazine.

Pharrell releases first single, "Can I Have it Like That?" featuring Gwen Stefani, from his debut solo album, *In My Mind.*

Pharrell teams with Japanese designer Nigo, and releases clothing labels Billionaire Boys Club and Ice Cream.

2006 Pharrell shoots "Say Somethin'" video with Mariah Carey in Paris.

Pharrell releases *In My Mind.*

Discography

2002　*In Search Of* (worldwide release), N.E.R.D.

2003　*The Neptunes Presents . . . Clones*, The Neptunes

2004　*Fly or Die*, N.E.R.D.

2006　*In My Mind*, Pharrell Williams

Award Nominations

2004　Black Entertainment Television's Best New Artist award

Black Entertainment Television's Best Collaboration award for "Frontin'," featuring Jay-Z

Awards

2001　Shortlist Music Prize for *In Search Of*

2002　The Source Awards Producers of the Year

Billboard Music Awards Producers of the Year

2004　Grammy Awards Producer of the Year, Non-Classical

Grammy Awards Best Pop Vocal Album for Justin Timberlake's *Justified*

2005　*Esquire* Magazine's Best Dressed Man in the World

Books

Chang, Jeff. *Can't Stop, Won't Stop: A History of the Hip-Hop Generation.* New York: St. Martin's Press, 2005.

Light, Alan. *The Vibe History of Hip-Hop.* New York: Three Rivers Press, 2001.

Waters, Rosa. *Hip-Hop: A Short History.* Broomall, PA: Mason Crest Publishers, 2007.

Magazines

Fiore, Raymond. "Pharrell: A Beautiful Mind." *Entertainment Weekly,* November 4, 2005.

Grazer, Brian. "Pharrell: He May Be Known for Making Hits, but Pharrell Williams Is More Interested in Breaking Down Walls." *Interview,* December 1, 2005.

Jackson, Michael. "Pharrell Williams: Music's Hottest Hitmaker Talks to the Thriller." *Interview,* August 1, 2003.

"Pharrell Tunes into Fashion." *WWD,* August 27, 2004.

"Pharrell's Day in the Sun," *WWD,* October 25, 2004.

Sutherland, Megan. "The Haunting of Pharrell Williams." *Paper,* February 1, 2004.

Tyrangiel, Josh. "Hip-Hop's Chic Geek: Whether Neptune, N.E.R.D., or Solo Star, Pharrell Williams Brings Sweetness to a Genre That Needs It." *Time,* August 25, 2003.

Web Sites

Pharrell Williams fan site
community.pharrellwilliams.com

Billionaire Boys Club and Ice Cream
www.bbcicecream.com

MTV Online
www.mtv.com

Official N.E.R.D. Web site
www.n-e-r-d.com

Star Trak Music's Web site
www.startrakmusic.com

VH1 Online
www.vh1.com

accolades—expressions of high praise.

activism—the direct and vigorous support on one side or the other of a controversial issue.

alter-ego—a second side to an individual's personality, different from the one most people know.

bastion—something regarded as providing strong defense or support, especially for a belief or cause, or a place where there are such people.

bling—big, bright, expensive jewelry.

debut—done for the first time.

disco—a popular dance music of the 1970s characterized by a strong beat.

DJ—disc jockey; someone who plays recorded music for the entertainment of others.

exclusive—limited to a select population.

formulaic—unoriginal and reliant on previous models or ideas.

funk—a type of music derived from jazz, blues, and soul, and characterized by a heavy rhythmic bass and backbeat.

id—the unconscious, the source of primitive instinctive impulses and drives.

improvisational—done in an unplanned manner.

innovative—new and original.

introspective—tending to make a detailed examination of someone's feelings, thoughts, and motives.

MC—emcee; someone who acts as a master of ceremonies.

mixer—a machine that takes multiple inputs and combines them to make a single output.

oratory—the art of public speaking.

paparazzi—freelance photographers who aggressively pursue celebrities for candid shots.

perfectionist—someone who demands perfection in all things.

platinum—signifying that an album has sold two million copies, or a single has sold one million copies.

producer—someone who organizes and supervises the creation of something.

R&B—rhythm and blues; a blending of jazz and the blues.

serendipitously—found in an unexpected manner.

soul—music that originated in African American gospel singing and is characterized by strong feeling and earthiness.

synthesizers—computerized electronic tools for producing and controlling sound.

uninhibited—free to act and feel spontaneously.

Terrell Brown believes in the power of language to shape the world. He hopes to use his writing to encourage young people to follow Pharrell's life motto: "Go for it." Terrell lives in upstate New York with his family and five pet goats.

Picture Credits

page

2: Marcocchi Giulio/Sipa Press
8: Jackson Lee/AdMedia
11: Zuma Press/Nancy Kaszerman
12: KRT/NMI
15: BSIP/Jack Griffin
16: Brian Prahl /Splash News
18: Zuma Press/Princess Anne High School
21: KRT/Frederic Nebinger
23: Ronald A/Big Pictures USA
24: Zuma Press/Marco Dos Santos/IXO
26: Zuma Press/Jodi Jones
29: KRT/Michael Perez

30: Jeff Steinberg/INFGoff
31: Zuma Press/Helena Kubicka
33: AFP/Hector Mata
35: Michelle Feng/NMI
36: Zuma Press/Dan Herrick-KPA
38: Kazuhiro Nogi/AFP/Getty Images
41: KRT/Lionel Hahn
43: Benoit Pujol /MaxPPP
44: Splash News
46: Zuma Press/Gary Lee/UPPA
49: BizWirePhotos/NMI
50: Zuma Press/Axel
53: WENN Photos
54: Chris Polk/FilmMagic

Front cover: Zach Lipp/AdMedia
Back cover: Zuma Press/Vaughn Youtz